I0441916

Sex partner

Evaluation of Behavior and Culture

Nigel Aksel

First Edition

Nigel Aksel
Sex Partner: Evaluation of Behavior and Culture, 2019

1st Edition
All Rights Reserved
ISBN: 9781077781498

Table of Content

Tables

Introduction

When matured, everyone looks for a person with an opposite gender for friendship, sex partnership or marriage.

It is normal and that's our human nature. But without norms and rules, and understanding of our ourselves, we will have difficulties.

This book is for those who look for, want to meet or plan to build a relationship with an opposite gender. It aims to help everyone, especially those who are meeting their sweethearts for the first time.

First, the book will help to understand both a behavior of the opposite gender and our own.

Second, the book provides valuable information to hook your sweetheart not only by words or social status, but also with the sense of humor and romance.

Third, a reader will learn how to make the first impression to your sweetheart, which make your relationship stronger and reliable.

Forth, anyone should know also the back side, especially how to avoid sexual harassment and sexual violence situations, no matter of the person's adores and temperament.

Fifth, the book explains how to build a long-term relationship based on understanding and promoting the idea of sharing responsibilities and roles.

Sixth, you should learn how to find a reliable, caring and the best match for your adventurous sex phantasies.

Finally, a reader will get many tips and cases to avoid difficult situations and do not miss great opportunities.

When your partner behaves or speak in a very negative way, many say that he or she is with bad culture. When your partner behaves and acts adequately, people around say that he or she has a very good values and culture. Evaluation of people generally will influence on the longevity of your relationships with your sex partner and generally your future.

The purpose of this book is to grow within you a sex culture for every situation, which will be well-accepted and moral in many ways. And it will help you make your sex life happier and long.

Lifecycle

It is important to start our book with a lifecycle to give you a sense of limitless of our all behaviors, love and adore and etc.

Let's check the following table to see the lifecycle of the human being and how limited our sex pre

Table 1 Lifecycle of Sex Partnership

Age (years)	Sex preference	Behavior to partner
1-13	Differentiate opposite gender, build trust to the same gender	Learning
14-25	Active interest in opposite gender, build trust to the opposite gender	Curious
25-40	High interest in opposite gender and sex	Adore
40-55	Interest in opposite gender and sex	Love

55-70	No interest in opposite gender and sex, interest in health	Relationship sharing
Above 70	Interest in health and medicines	Support

From the table, we can see that our sex preferences and behavior in regard to partner have some limited time scale. And there is no understanding that the sex can continue forever and unlimited.

Young people, especially at the age 12-16 can do a lot of mistakes and build different illusions about the sex partner and unlimited adore and love.

But in many cases, this can influence their lives and careers and sometimes their future.

The table 1 shows that we have to plan our life in the best way to do everything in time, with the right pace and partner.

For example, I have many friends at 40, who are still alone or not married and they are still looking for. They do not understand that their human body is getting older and older and now they have several issues.

First, the ladies of their age look very old for them. Second, the ladies of younger age look beautiful but they prefer younger man as their partners for sex or life.

So, the table 1 tells us that everything should be in time in our life.

Moreover, table 1 shows that our behavior changes with time. When you are at 40 and you are waiting a love from a partner, your young sex partner at 25 maybe just want some sex with you. And she might be thinking that at 40 you want sex also, but it is not purely true. You want probably the same, but you look for a true love.

So, in this regard, many people who want to try marry at older ages to younger partners are in the wrong conclusion.

Therefore, in many cases, these relationships or marriages are not long-term or last for few years.

Tips:

1) Check your sex lifecycle
2) Understand your age and behavior
3) Plan you sex relationships for your life

Behavior

Our behavior is so different and we behave differently for the same situations. Our sex behaviors depend on many factors. The main factors are:

1) Character
2) Education
3) Experience
4) Knowledge and Information
5) Psychology
6) Finance
7) Social status
8) Culture
9) Others

For understanding the behavior of your sex partner, it is important that you evaluate many factors of the behavior of your sex partner.

For example, a leadership character can be a natural or based on sex preferences to you. If you see that he has a leadership character only in front of you than it is a big problem. He will try to his muscles or character in future.

In case your sex partner is handsome but without sex education you will be also in the row of those who will be dissatisfied. Without sex education, it will be difficult to achieve the adore and orgasm during your sex plays.

The most dangerous are those partners, who are ready to give the last coin to share a bed with a sex partner. They will try to show off as a rich man, but after they satisfied, they will dilute the expectations of the sex partner.

There is a question: what is the best behavior for your sex partner without any inclination from the norm of moral and harassment?

The answer is not simple. It depends on your gender and many other factors above. Moreover, there are also circumstances such as period of relationship, intentions from relationship, first meeting or a long relationship case etc.

Therefore, let's classify some appropriate and non-appropriate behaviors for man and women in the table 2 below.

Table 2 Appropriate and Non-appropriate Behaviors

	Men	Women
Appropriate behavior	-Approach diligently, with respect and smile -Respect lady's choice and answer -Offers to go to cinema, theater	-Act openly, curious and testifying -Be polite -Support the talk -Ask questions

	or other interesting places	
Non-appropriate behavior	-Offers alcohol or cigar -Offers a kiss or sex -Push lady for alcohol or cigar -Show the muscles -Offend your partner	-Seduces man with body parts -Offers alcohol or cigar -Offers a kiss or sex -Scold and be negative about people

Table 2 shows many appropriate and non-appropriate behaviors, especially for the first date or time.

Generally, in order to be successful with your sex partner in relationship building, you have to learn how to behave in different situations and meetings.

Tips:

1) Understand your and your partner's behavior
2) Act appropriately with respect to your sex partner
3) Learn how to behave in different situations

Sex Partner

During my lifetime, I was asking many men and women what are their ideal partners for life. Even here, men and women answered differently.

For example, younger matured boys were saying sexy and attractive girl, mid-age men were saying a reliable and caring partner, and old men were saying healthy and intelligent women.

The same was for ladies.

Let me briefly show it on the table 3 based on my personal observations.

Table 3 Preferences of men and women

	Preferences of Men	Preferences of Women
14-25	-sexy and attractive -chatty	-masculine and attractive -cocky
25-40	-reliable and caring -tactful	-kind, intelligent and supportive -brave
Above 40	-healthy and intelligent -household	-non-drinker, honest and reliable -skillful

The table 3 shows a very important lesson that with years, preferences of men and women in opposite sex changes dramatically.

If a young person understands this as early as possible, he will focus to learn values and character of the opposite sex to understand what to expert in future. If he or she understands that expectations for the future is not satisfied then he or she will stop their relationships as early as possible.

Similarly, it is important for understanding person's own preferences.

For example, why we look for an opposite sex. To date or chat, to have a sex or to marry, to share or learn.

After living with your sex partner for a long year, your preferences are also changing. Especially if you started to breed your kids or your financial source changed.

When you read the book from the beginning till the end, you will be able to understand many details of the person's psychology and focus on long-term goals of your future. Not alone but with your sex or lifelong partner.

You understand that together with your partner it is much easier to plan and live the life. But it is to plan your future not alone, but with your partner. In this way, you can achieve your goals in full and harmony.

Tips:

1) Understand the preferences of your and your sex partner
2) Focus on long-term goals for life with your sex partner and learn how to plan your future together

Next, let's to see about planning.

Planning

The most important skill of the human beings is planning. It helped to achieve many goals in their lives and brought technological revolution we know can see and live.

Without planning – nothing is possible to achieve effectively.

However, not all plans are achievable and it depends on your skills and scopes of thinking.

Planning requires also learning, trying, testing, acting, analyzing and many other activities.

So, please, do not think that planning is a simple task and after planning you will achieve everything. It is not true, unfortunately.

Another point, we have 3 main planning for our successful life with sex partner.

First, planning of your behavior.

Second, planning of your sex partner.

Third, planning of your life, i.e. future.

For example, planning your behavior requires a lot of training of yourself. Planning of your sex partner requires a lot of analysis and comparisons. Planning of your life and future, requires a wide scope of analysis, capabilities, skills and many other factors.

To make it simple, let's start with planning of your behavior. It is actually your character building not only for your sex partner, but also for many other interests and activities in life.

To illustrate, let's see in the following table to understand the scope of planning the behavior.

Table 4 Areas of Learning Personal Behavior

	Personal Natural Behavior	Responsive Behavior	Defensive or Attack Behavior
Analysis	yes	yes	
Verbal Communication	yes	yes	yes
Non-verbal communication	yes	yes	yes
Physical training	yes	yes	yes
Psychology		yes	
Art of defense and attack (marshal art)			yes
Sexology		yes	
Anatomy		yes	
Medicine			yes

Table 4 shows many areas for your learning to understand the behavior of yourself in very different situations.

First, you have to learn how to be a natural person or at least look natural in various situations. And, in the table you can see that you have to develop your verbal and non-verbal communication skills for that.

For example, you have to look naturally strong when someone tries to harass you. And if you show that you are a weak person, your potential sex partner can hurt you or will act aggressively, especially in cases if your partner is drunk or under the excitement.

Another case, when you like the person and you started your relationship. In this case, you have to learn how to respond your partner in the most appropriate way. And you have to understand that your partner is also evaluating you for partnership for life or for one night. This requires certain skills to understand your partner's intentions and your feelings also.

The best match comes after 100% of suitability.

At point, let's brief on planning of your sex partner.

So, let's see the table 5 to understand the factors for selection of your sex partner.

Table 5 Traditional Factors for Evaluation of Your Sex Partner

Sexuality Factors	Evaluation	Level	Professional Factors
Appearance			Education
Nationality			Experience
Horoscope			Social status
Character			Skills
Sex Education			Income level
Sex Experience			Interests
Height			Hobbies
Weight			Plans
Blood Group			Languages
Family			Research
Friends			Achievements
Genetics			Medals
Ethnicity			Certificates
Medical history			Awards

Table 5 shows that people evaluate their partners for sex based on many factors - personal and professional.

There is no single or correct answer, which one is the best one. But this traditional way of evaluating your sex partner create many wrong illusions and imaginations.

The main point that people do not evaluate their partners based on responsibilities. Let's check the following table for planning your sex partner for a long-term relationship.

Table 6 Factors for evaluating and planning your sex partner

Responsibility Areas and Factors	For you	For your partner	Together
Shopping			
Cooking			
Breeding			
House work			
Payments			
Traveling			
Family budget			
Children Education, Sports and others			
Outdoor activities			
Books			
Family business			
Driving			
Cleaning			
Washing			
Garbage and wastes			
Parents			
Garden			
Pets			

Table 6 shows that you have to understand factors and who will be responsible for them.

Imagine a situation when you and your partner cannot cook. It can create a bad experience for your life and become a case for your conflicts, no matter how you were the best match in traditional way of evaluation.

The same for payments, if both of you unemployed or cannot support your activities, travelling or dinners, you are going to be bored very fast from your sex partner.

So, for a healthy sex relationship you have to understand your responsibility areas and factors very well.

The last point of planning is planning for your life and future. It is most difficult as no one can predict your future in advance.

But, if you can plan it in the way that what to do in 5 or 10 or 50 years, you will be motivated to achieve those goal together with your sex partner.

That is because, you have many other factors that you have to take into consideration while you want to spend your time with your sex partner, especially for long term success.

Life is limited and you have to learn and plan your life goals and future appropriately. Every missed day or month or year can destroy your long-term happiness and put much more efforts to find your life balance.

To be to the point of the aim of the book, let's see the main factors for planning your life and future in the table 7.

Table 7 Life and future plans

Life and future plans	Responsibility	Results
Bringing and breeding your kids	Together	Helps to strengthen the partnership
Building/Purchasing a House/Car/etc.	Together	Assist your life, foundation for your offspring
Educate your children and yourself	Together	Build healthy and smart offspring and future
Start your family business	Together	Support family goals and kids
Travel to new destinations		Expand horizons of yourself and your kids
Donate and educate others	Together	Help orphans and poorer to grow
Practice religion and learn new religion practices	Together	Balance your internal energy and soil
Become a global citizen	Together	Learn and share new ideas

Table 7 shows some of the main goals for life and future planning for both you and your sex partner. It will strengthen your relationships, trust and life-long stamina.

To illustrate, I noticed that most of the successful family plan their family business from the starting point. They share, learn and do together the new common business together.

Another example is with religion. My observations show that families, including secular and modern values, which practice religion are those with strong relationship values.

Religion helps to avoid the most usual life mistakes such as violation of human laws, including betrayal, jealousy and adultery etc.

It also keeps partners from interest in homosexual, pedophilia and other abnormal behaviors or sex activities.

Therefore, planning life-long and future goals with your sex partner can help build a long-lasting relationship based on trust, love and mutual understanding.

Tips:

1) Explore and improve your personal behavior to be demanding, interesting and responsive for any life-long case;
2) Understand traditional factors to evaluate your sex partner and avoid misunderstandings or wrong illusions.
3) Learn how to evaluate your common responsibilities with your sex partner to find the best match;
4) Focus on your common life-long and future plans to build long-lasting relationships.

Best Qualities

Many of my friends and girlfriends who were single and who wanted to build their first relationship were asking me many times, what the main qualities to have for your date or first meetings.

From my own experience and 10 years of marriage, I can underline several of them.

Firstly, it is sense of humor. It is a positive character and it is not about knowing or ability to tell anecdotes or funny stories. It is more about how to make any talk with your sex partner funny and interesting, continuing with passion and splashing connections.

Secondly, it is about sense of romance. Being romantic is not only about saying something romantic, it is also about how to create an imagination of romance, an atmosphere of love, care and respect. For example, if you invited a sex partner for a dinner and you have only read your special poem, it will be romantic, but it might not create an imagination of romance.

The main attributes or conditions for creating a romantic atmosphere and imagination in your sex partner are:

1) Unusual flowers such as rose, tulip or orchid;
2) Chocolate;
3) Wine or Champaign;
4) Candles;
5) Unusual and tasty food;
6) Romantic music;
7) Dance;
8) Unusual place (top of the mountain or skyscraper with beautiful view);
9) Seashore or river bank;
10) Cool and tasty dessert etc.

Thirdly, a sense of care. No matter you are a man or woman, if you learn how to show your care to your sex partner, you can be sure that you can grow your relationship in the right direction.

To be careful is not about asking your partner every 5 minute a question about his health or call him/her. To be careful is understanding your partner's internal world and external condition and offer your best support or words. Your support can be simple, just sentence of words with hug or something like that. But it should be to the point of the topic which disturbs your partner at the moment.

Moreover, a sense of care has many other positive features and attributes, such as:

1) A care about pets;
2) A care about plants;
3) A care about children;
4) A care about environment etc.

Fourthly, sense of responsibility. I have already mentioned about the responsibility.

Responsibility has its own attributes and conditions. Let me count some of them below.

1) A person of word, i.e. trustworthy;
2) A person of time, i.e. punctual;
3) A reliable person;
4) A control of yourself;
5) A control of emotions;
6) Fairness;
7) Decisive for actions;
8) Defensive of common interests etc.

There are many attributes of the responsible person indeed. And responsibility grows from family stories and movies in the childhood. It is not a one-day attribute in fact.

Fifthly, communicative skills. Today, communication skills are the most important part for harmonic dialogue. It is not about talking all the time without non-stop. It is about understanding many attributes and features of communication such as:

1) When to say or not about the story/case;

2) When to interrupt and when not;
3) Understanding verbal and non-verbal languages;
4) When to say complements;
5) When to stop the topic of discussion etc.
6) Understanding the feelings and emotions and communicating appropriately etc.

In relationships, even misleading small text or electronic message can hurt your sex partner and stop your relationship forever.

Therefore, it is important to talk with your sex partner on various psychological conditions of your communication. For example, explain your sex partner how to calm down you when you are nervous or too angry. You can even make your mesmerizing words to say each other to calm down in difficult situations.

Sixthly, a sense of confidence. I am not sure that it is the best quality, but I personally believe that a confidence comes after your experience or learning the topic, situation and case.

Confidence of you and your partner will help to build effective communication based on trust, responsibility and long-term orientation.

The attributes of confidence are:

1) Knowledge;
2) Experience;

3) Leadership;
4) Responsibility;
5) Openness;
6) Supportiveness etc.

Tips:

1) Learn how to form your best qualities for your long-lasting sex partnership;
2) Use various attributes and conditions of best qualities;
3) Evaluate the qualities of your partner and compare with yourself.
4) Assess the qualities of your sex partner and check them how they match to your plans, including life-long and future.

Culture

We live in a global environment with our own cultural values and traditions. In many countries, local cultural values and traditions are a serious barrier for sex relationship building and happy life satisfaction.

For example, in some traditional cultures, your parents find your life-long sex partner based on evaluation of traditional factors (Table 5) and in some cultures, you have to steal your bride to marry and build your future as a man.

The book aims to uncover the topic in many parts of the world and help people to build a new culture in regard to sex partner.

What are main features and attributes of the sex culture in today's global environment.

Let me count some of the main one below:

1) Gender Equality;
2) Control of Emotions;
3) Don't raise a hand to a woman;
4) Put appropriate cloth;
5) Control the birth rate of your family;
6) Plan your sex partnership and future;
7) Avoid violations and insults of partners based on social statuses, nationality, ethnicity etc.

8) Cultivate the happiness of man and woman via growing children;
9) Human Rights Protection;
10) Child Rights Protection etc.

Tips:

1) Spread new global values and traditions for sex partnership
2) Cultivate a global culture within your family values and traditions

Ask yourself

After the reading the sections above analyze yourself and how you react to the behavior of your partner, answer yourself to the following questions:

1) Is it easy for me to evaluate and find my sex partner?
2) Do I want long-term relationship or short term?
3) Do I know my cultural values and traditions?
4) Do I know what I want from my partner?
5) Do I learn how to react, defend or act in various situations with my sex partner?
6) Do I know who is my ideal sex partner?

If you answer "no" to all questions above, it is important to think over yourself and your plans over finding your partner. And if you did not read the book, please try to read it and understand the ideas and tips. It will help you to answer questions with more positive "yes".

In conclusion, it is important to point it out that if you learn how to control your sex partnership, you will be able to control your long-lasting relationships and future.

Conclusion

This book is the beginning of disclosure of key topics of our everyday relationships, between man and woman, between people of various nations, ethnical groups, religion etc.

As a author I will be happy to see your comments and ideas how I can improve my first books on this important issue of today's global agenda.

Please send me your messages via email at: innoker@gmail.com

About author

Nigel Aksel is a farther of 3 kids and a global citizen with more than 20 years of experience in research of social and personal behavior. He is involved as a lecturer of marketing and management at the South-Kazakhstan State University.

Nigel enjoys writing about multiple issues of the social, cultural and economic development. As a member of educational institutions, he understands well about the problems of nations and their development. He explores many areas on how to develop our global culture to help people around the world to adapt to the international level and new global moral standards.

Notes and Memories

Nurbek Achilov has some resources for you!

On Blogger's platform he runs his blog about investments, export, trade and other issues.

Blog about investment, export and trade in English:

https://nurbekachilov.blogspot.com/

Blog about investment, export and trade in English:

https://nurbekachil.blogspot.com/

You can also find ideas, photos and experiences about investments, trade and investment on Nurbek Achilov's pages in Facebook, Instagram, Pinterest, Slideshare,

Academia and LinkedIn and other accounts.

orcid.org/0000-0003-1238-6556

Kazakhstan

Tips for Travelers

Nurbek Achilov

Second Edition

Get my new book with the Special Price on
Amazon.com

200 web-sites and tools for online presence

Essential Handbook for marketing and growth

Nurbek Achilov

First Edition

Get the Second Edition with the Special Price on
Amazon.com

Event Management

Tips and strategies

Nigel Aksel

Second Edition

Order my newest book with the Special Price on
Amazon.com

Global Citizen

Thinking Beyond

Nurbek Achilov

First Edition